Mac Flecknoe and Other Poems

John Dryden

Mac Flecknoe and Other Poems

Table of Contents

Mac Flecknoe and Other Poems

John Dryden

ABSALOM AND ACHITOPHEL: A POEM

In pious times, ere priest–craft did begin,
Before polygamy was made a sin;
When man, on many, multipli'd his kind,
Ere one to one was cursedly confin'd:
When Nature prompted, and no Law deni'd
Promiscuous use of concubine and bride;
Then, Israel's monarch, after Heaven's own heart,
His vigorous warmth did variously impart
To wives and slaves: and, wide as his command,
Scatter'd his Maker's image through the land.
Michal, of royal blood, the crown did wear;
A soil ungrateful to the tiller's care:
Not so the rest; for several mothers bore
To god–like David, several sons before.
But since like slaves his bed they did ascend,
No true succession could their seed attend.
Of all this numerous progeny was none
So beautiful, so brave, as Absalom:
Whether, inspir'd by some diviner lust,
His father got him with a greater gust;
Or that his conscious destiny made way,
By manly beauty to imperial sway.
Early in foreign fields he won renown,

With kings and states alli'd to Israel's crown:
In peace the thoughts of war he could remove,
And seem'd as he were only born for love.
Whate'er he did, was done with so much ease,
In him alone, 'twas natural to please:
His motions all accompani'd with grace;
And Paradise was open'd in his face.
With secret joy, indulgent David view'd
His youthful image in his son renew'd:
To all his wishes nothing he deni'd;
And made the charming Annabel his bride.
What faults he had (for who from faults is free?)
His father could not, or he would not see.
Some warm excesses, which the Law forbore,
Were constru'd youth that purged by boiling o'er:
And Amnon's murther, by a specious name,
Was call'd a just revenge for injur'd fame.
Thus prais'd, and lov'd, the noble youth remain'd,
While David, undisturb'd, in Sion reign'd.
But life can never be sincerely blest:
Heav'n punishes the bad, and proves the best.
The Jews, a headstrong, moody, murm'ring race,
As ever tri'd th'extent and stretch of grace;
God's pamper'd people whom, debauch'd with ease,
No king could govern, nor no God could please;
(Gods they had tri'd of every shape and size,
That god–smiths could produce, or priests devise:)
These Adam–wits, too fortunately free,
Began to dream they wanted liberty:
And when no rule, no precedent, was found
Of men, by laws less circumscrib'd and bound,
They led their wild desires to woods and caves,
And thought that all but savages were slaves.
They who, when Saul was dead, without a blow,
Made foolish Ishbosheth the crown forego;
Who banisht David did from Hebron bring,

And, with a general shout, proclaim'd him king:
Those very Jews, who, at their very best,
Their Humour more than loyalty exprest,
Now, wonder'd why, so long, they had obey'd
An idol—monarch which their hands had made:
Thought they might ruin him they could create;
Or melt him to that golden calf, a state.
But these were random bolts: no form'd design,
Nor interest made the factious crowd to join:
The sober part of Israel, free from stain,
Well knew the value of a peaceful reign:
And, looking backward with a wise afright,
Saw seams of wounds, dishonest to the sight:
In contemplation of whose ugly scars,
They curst the memory of civil wars.
The moderate sort of men, thus qualifi'd,
Inclin'd the balance to the better side:
And, David's mildness manag'd it so well,
The bad found no occasion to rebel.
But, when to sin our bias'd nature leans,
The careful Devil is still at hand with means;
And providently pimps for ill desires:
The good old cause reviv'd, a plot requires.
Plots, true or false, are necessary things,
To raise up common—wealths, and ruin kings.

Th' inhabitants of old Jerusalem
Were Jebusites: the town so call'd from them;
And theirs the native right—
But when the chosen people grew more strong,
The rightful cause at length became the wrong:
And every loss the men of Jebus bore,
They still were thought God's enemies the more.
Thus, worn and weaken'd, well or ill content,
Submit they must to David's government:
Impoverish'd and depriv'd of all command,

Their taxes doubled as they lost their land;
And, what was harder yet to flesh and blood,
Their gods disgrac'd, and burnt like common wood.
This set the heathen priesthood in a flame;
For priests of all religions are the same:
Of whatsoe'er descent their godhead be,
Stock, stone, or other homely pedigree,
In his defence his servants are as bold,
As if he had been born of beaten gold.
The Jewish Rabbins though their Enemies,
In this conclude them honest men and wise:
For 'twas their duty, all the learned think,
T'espouse his cause by whom they eat and drink.
From hence began that plot, the nation's curse,
Bad in itself, but represented worse.
Rais'd in extremes, and in extremes decri'd;
With oaths affirm'd, with dying vows deni'd.
Not weigh'd, or winnow'd by the multitude;
But swallow'd in the mass, unchew'd and crude.
Some truth there was, but dash'd and brew'd with lies;
To please the fools, and puzzle all the wise.
Succeeding times did equal folly call,
Believing nothing, or believing all.
Th' Egyptian rites the Jebusites embrac'd;
Where gods were recommended by their taste.
Such sav'ry deities must needs be good,
As serv'd at once for worship and for food.
By force they could not introduce these gods;
For ten to one, in former days was odds.
So fraud was us'd, (the sacrificers' trade,)
Fools are more hard to conquer than persuade.
Their busy teachers mingled with the Jews;
And rak'd, for converts, even the court and stews:
Which Hebrew priests the more unkindly took,
Because the fleece accompanies the flock.
Some thought they God's anointed meant to slay

4

By guns, invented since full many a day:
Our author swears it not; but who can know
How far the Devil and Jebusites may go?
This plot, which fail'd for want of common sense,
Had yet a deep and dangerous consequence:
For, as when raging fevers boil the blood,
The standing lake soon floats into a flood;
And ev'ry hostile humour, which before
Slept quiet in its channels, bubbles o'er:
So, several factions from this first ferment,
Work up to foam, and threat the government.
Some by their friends, more by themselves thought wise,
Oppos'd the pow'r, to which they could not rise.
Some had in courts been great, and thrown from thence,
Like fiends, were harden'd in impenitence.
Some by their monarch's fatal mercy grown,
From pardon'd rebels, kinsmen to the throne;
Were rais'd in pow'r and public office high;
Strong bands, if bands ungrateful men could tie.

Of these the false Achitophel was first:
A name to all succeeding ages curst.
For close designs, and crooked counsels fit;
Sagacious, bold and turbulent of wit:
Restless, unfixt in principles and place;
In pow'r unpleas'd, impatient of disgrace.
A fiery soul, which working out its way,
Fretted the pigmy—body to decay:
And o'er inform'd the tenement of clay.
A daring pilot in extremity;
Pleas'd with the danger, when the waves went high
He sought the storms; but for a calm unfit,
Would steer too nigh the sands, to boast his wit.
Great wits are sure to madness near alli'd;
And thin partitions do their bounds divide:
Else, why should he, with wealth and honour blest,

5

Refuse his age the needful hours of rest?
Punish a body which he could not please;
Bankrupt of life, yet prodigal of ease?
And all to leave, what with his toil he won
To that unfeather'd, two–legg'd thing, a son:
Got, while his soul did huddled notions try;
And born a shapeless lump, like anarchy.
In friendship false, implacable in hate:
Resolv'd to ruin or to rule the state.
To compass this, the triple bond he broke;
The pillars of the public safety shook:
And fitted Israel for a foreign yoke.
Then, seiz'd with fear, yet still affecting fame,
Usurp'd a patriot's all–atoning name.
So easy still it proves in factious times,
With public zeal to cancel private crimes:
How safe is treason, and how sacred ill,
Where none can sin against the people's will:
Where crowds can wink; and no offence be known,
Since in another's guilt they find their own.
Yet, fame deserv'd, no enemy can grudge;
The statesman we abhor, but praise the judge.
In Jewish courts ne'er sat an Abbethdin
With more discerning eyes, or hands more clean:
Unbrib'd, unsought, the wretched to redress;
Swift of dispatch, and easy of access.
Oh, had he been content to serve the crown,
With virtues only proper to the gown;
Or, had the rankness of the soil been freed
From cockle, that opprest the noble seed:
David, for him his tuneful harp had strung,
And heav'n had wanted one immortal song.
But wild ambition loves to slide, not stand;
And fortune's ice prefers to virtue's land:
Achitophel, grown weary to possess
A lawful fame, and lazy happiness;

6

Disdain'd the golden fruit to gather free,
And lent the crowd his arm to shake the tree.
Now, manifest of crimes, contriv'd long since,
He stood at bold defiance with his prince:
Held up the buckler of the people's cause,
Against the crown; and skulk'd behind the laws.
The wish'd occasion of the plot he takes;
Some circumstances finds, but more he makes.
By buzzing emissaries, fills the ears
Of list'ning crowds, with jealousies and fears
Of arbitrary counsels brought to light,
And proves the king himself a Jebusite.
Weak arguments! which yet he knew full well,
Were strong with people easy to rebel.
For, govern'd by the moon, the giddy Jews
Tread the same track when she the prime renews:
And once in twenty years, their scribes record,
By natural instinct they change their lord.
Achitophel still wants a chief, and none
Was found so fit as warlike Absalom:
Not, that he wish'd his greatness to create,
(For politicians neither love nor hate:)
But, for he knew, his title not allow'd,
Would keep him still depending on the crowd:
That kingly pow'r, thus ebbing out, might be
Drawn to the dregs of a democracy.
Him he attempts, with studied arts to please,
And sheds his venom, in such words as these.

Auspicious Prince! at whose nativity
Some royal planet rul'd the southern sky;
Thy longing country's darling and desire;
Their cloudy pillar, and their guardian fire:
Their second Moses, whose extended wand
Divides the seas, and shows the promis'd land:
Whose dawning day, in very distant age,

7

Has exercis'd the sacred prophet's rage:
The people's pray'r, the glad diviner's theme,
The young men's vision, and the old men's dream!
Thee, Saviour, thee, the nation's vows confess;
And, never satisfi'd with seeing, bless:
Swift, unbespoken pomps, thy steps proclaim,
And stammering babes are taught to lisp thy name.
How long wilt thou the general joy detain;
Starve, and defraud the people of thy reign?
Content ingloriously to pass thy days
Like one of virtue's fools that feeds on praise;
Till thy fresh glories, which now shine so bright,
Grow stale and tarnish with our daily sight.
Believe me, royal youth, thy fruit must be,
Or gather'd ripe, or rot upon the tree.
Heav'n has to all allotted, soon or late,
Some lucky revolution of their fate:
Whose motions if we watch and guide with skill,
(For human good depends on human will,)
Our fortune rolls, as from a smooth descent,
And, from the first impression, takes the bent:
But, if unseiz'd, she glides away like wind;
And leaves repenting folly far behind.
Now, now she meets you, with a glorious prize,
And spreads her locks before her as she flies.
Had thus Old David, from whose loins you spring,
Not dar'd, when fortune call'd him, to be king.
At Gath an exile he might still remain;
And Heaven's anointing oil had been in vain.
Let his successful youth your hopes engage;
But shun th'example of declining age:
Behold him setting in his western skies,
The shadows lengthening as the vapours rise.
He is not now, as when on Jordan's sand
The joyful people throng'd to see him land,
Cov'ring the beach, and black'ning all the strand:

But, like the Prince of Angels from his height,
Comes tumbling downward with diminish'd light:
Betray'd by one poor plot to public scorn:
(Our only blessing since his curst return:)
Those heaps of people which one sheaf did bind,
Blown off, and scatter'd by a puff of wind.
What strength can he to your designs oppose,
Naked of friends and round beset with foes?
If Pharaoh's doubtful succour he should use,
A foreign aid would more incense the Jews:
Proud Egypt would dissembled friendship bring;
Foment the war, but not support the king:
Nor would the royal party e'er unite
With Pharaoh's arms, t'assist the Jebusite;
Or if they should, their interest soon would break,
And with such odious aid, make David weak.
All sorts of men, by my successful arts,
Abhorring kings, estrange their alter'd hearts
From David's rule: And 'tis the general Cry,
Religion, Common–wealth, and Liberty.
If, you, as champion of the public good,
Add to their arms a chief of royal blood;
What may not Israel hope, and what applause
Might such a general gain by such a cause?
Not barren praise alone, that gaudy flow'r,
Fair only to the sight, but solid pow'r:
And nobler is a limited command,
Giv'n by the love of all your native land,
Than a successive title, long, and dark,
Drawn from the mouldy rolls of Noah's Ark.

What cannot praise effect in mighty minds,
When flattery soothes, and when ambition blinds!
Desire of pow'r, on earth a vicious weed,
Yet, sprung from high, is of celestial seed:
In God 'tis glory: And when men aspire,

'Tis but a spark too much of heavenly fire.
Th' ambitious youth, too covetous of fame,
Too full of angel's metal in his frame;
Unwarily was led from virtue's ways;
Made drunk with honour, and debauch'd with praise.
Half loath, and half consenting to the ill,
(For loyal blood within him struggled still)
He thus repli'd.—And what pretence have I
To take up arms for public liberty?
My Father governs with unquestion'd right;
The Faith's defender, and mankind's delight:
Good, gracious, just, observant of the laws;
And Heav'n by wonders has espous'd his cause.
Whom has he wrong'd in all his peaceful reign?
Who sues for justice to his throne in vain?
What millions has he pardon'd of his foes,
Whom just revenge did to his wrath expose?
Mild, easy, humble, studious of our good;
Inclin'd to mercy, and averse from blood.
If mildness ill with stubborn Israel suit,
His crime is God's beloved attribute.
What could he gain, his people to betray,
Or change his right, for arbitrary sway?
Let haughty Pharaoh curse with such a reign,
His fruitful Nile, and yoke a servile train.
If David's rule Jerusalem displease,
The Dog–star heats their brains to this disease.
Why then should I, encouraging the bad,
Turn rebel, and run popularly mad?
Were he a tyrant who, by lawless might,
Oppress'd the Jews, and rais'd the Jebusite,
Well might I mourn; but nature's holy bands
Would curb my spirits, and restrain my hands:
The people might assert their liberty;
But what was right in them, were crime in me.
His favour leaves me nothing to require;

Prevents my wishes, and out–runs desire.
What more can I expect while David lives?
All but his kingly diadem he gives:
And that: but there he paus'd; then sighing, said,
Is justly destin'd for a worthier head.
For when my father from his toils shall rest,
And late augment the number of the blest:
His lawful issue shall the throne ascend;
Or the collat'ral line where that shall end.
His brother, though oppress'd with vulgar spite,
Yet dauntless and secure of native right,
Of every royal virtue stands possess'd;
Still dear to all the bravest, and the best.
His courage foes, his friends his truth proclaim;
His loyalty the king, the world his fame.
His mercy ev'n th'offending crowd will find:
For sure he comes of a forgiving kind.
Why should I then repine at Heaven's decree;
Which gives me no pretence to royalty?
Yet oh that Fate, propitiously inclin'd,
Had rais'd my birth, or had debas'd my mind;
To my large soul, not all her treasure lent,
And then betray'd it to a mean descent.
I find, I find my mounting spirits bold,
And David's part disdains my mother's mold.
Why am I scanted by a niggard–birth?
My soul disclaims the kindred of her earth:
And made for empire, whispers me within;
Desire of greatness is a god–like sin.

Him staggering so when Hell's dire agent found,
While fainting virtue scarce maintain'd her ground,
He pours fresh forces in, and thus replies:

Th'eternal God, supremely good and wise,
Imparts not these prodigious gifts in vain;

What wonders are reserv'd to bless your reign?
Against your will your arguments have shown,
Such virtue's only giv'n to guide a throne.
Not that your father's mildness I contemn;
But manly force becomes the diadem.
'Tis true, he grants the people all they crave;
And more perhaps than subjects ought to have:
For lavish grants suppose a monarch tame,
And more his goodness than his wit proclaim.
But when should people strive their bonds to break,
If not when kings are negligent or weak?
Let him give on till he can give no more,
The thrifty Sanhedrin shall keep him poor:
And every shekel which he can receive,
Shall cost a limb of his prerogative.
To ply him with new plots, shall be my care;
Or plunge him deep in some expensive war;
Which, when his treasure can no more supply,
He must, with the remains of kingship, buy.
His faithful friends, our jealousies and fears
Call Jebusites; and Pharaoh's pensioners:
Whom, when our fury from his aid has torn,
He shall be naked left to public scorn.
The next successor, whom I fear and hate,
My arts have made obnoxious to the state;
Turn'd all his virtues to his overthrow,
And gain'd our elders to pronounce a foe.
His right, for sums of necessary gold,
Shall first be pawn'd, and afterwards be sold:
Till time shall ever–wanting David draw,
To pass your doubtful title into law:
If not; the people have a right supreme
To make their kings; for kings are made for them.
All empire is no more than pow'r in trust:
Which when resum'd, can be no longer just.
Succession, for the general good design'd,

In its own wrong a nation cannot bind:
If altering that, the people can relieve,
Better one suffer, than a nation grieve.
The Jews well know their pow'r: ere Saul they chose,
God was their king, and God they durst depose.
Urge now your piety, your filial name,
A father's right, and fear of future fame;
The public good, the universal call,
To which even Heav'n submitted, answers all.
Nor let his love enchant your generous mind;
'Tis Nature's trick to propagate her kind.
Our fond begetters, who would never die,
Love but themselves in their posterity.
Or let his kindness by th'effects be tri'd,
Or let him lay his vain pretence aside.
God said he lov'd your father; could he bring
A better proof, than to anoint him king?
It surely show'd he lov'd the shepherd well,
Who gave so fair a flock as Israel.
Would David have you thought his darling son?
What means he then, to alienate the crown?
The name of godly he may blush to bear:
'Tis after God's own heart to cheat his heir.
He to his brother gives supreme command;
To you a legacy of barren land:
Perhaps th'old harp, on which he thrums his lays:
Or some dull Hebrew ballad in your praise.
Then the next heir, a prince, severe and wise
Already looks on you with jealous eyes;
Sees through the thin disguises of your arts,
And marks your progress in the people's hearts.
Though now his mighty soul in grief contains,
He meditates revenge who least complains;
And like a lion, slumb'ring in the way,
Or sleep–dissembling, while he waits his prey,
His fearless foes within his distance draws;

Constrains his roaring and contracts his paws:
Till at the last, his time for fury found,
He shoots with sudden vengeance from the ground:
The prostrate vulgar, passes o'er, and spares;
But with a lordly rage, his hunters tears.
Your case no tame expedients will afford;
Resolve on death, or conquest by the sword,
Which for no less a stake than life, you draw;
And self–defence is Nature's eldest law.
Leave the warm people no considering time;
For then rebellion may be thought a crime.
Prevail yourself of what occasion gives,
But try your title while your father lives:
And that your arms may have a fair pretence,
Proclaim, you take them in the king's defence:
Whose sacred life each minute would expose
To plots from seeming friends and secret foes.
And who can sound the depth of David's soul?
Perhaps his fear, his kindness may control.
He fears his brother, though he loves his son,
For plighted vows too late to be undone.
If so, by force he wishes to be gain'd;
Like women's lechery, to seem constrain'd:
Doubt not; but when he most affects the frown,
Commit a pleasing rape upon the crown.
Secure his person to secure your cause;
They who possess the prince, possess the laws.

He said, and this advice above the rest
With Absalom's mild nature suited best;
Unblam'd of life, (ambition set aside,)
Not stain'd with cruelty, nor puff'd with pride.
How happy had he been, if destiny
Had higher plac'd his birth, or not so high!
His kingly virtues might have claim'd a throne;
And blest all other countries but his own:

But charming greatness since so few refuse,
'Tis juster to lament him, than accuse.
Strong were his hopes a rival to remove,
With blandishments to gain the public love;
To head the faction while their zeal was hot,
And popularly prosecute the plot.
To farther this Achitophel unites
The malcontents of all the Israelites:
Whose differing parties he could wisely join,
For several ends, to serve the same design.
The best, and of the princes some were such,
Who thought the pow'r of monarchy too much:
Mistaken men, and patriots in their hearts;
Not wicked, but seduc'd by impious arts.
By these the springs of property were bent,
And wound so high, they crack'd the government.
The next for interest sought t'embroil the state,
To sell their duty at a dearer rate;
And make their Jewish markets of the throne;
Pretending public good, to serve their own.
Others thought kings an useless heavy load,
Who cost too much, and did too little good.
These were for laying honest David by,
On principles of pure good husbandry.
With them join'd all th'haranguers of the throng,
That thought to get preferment by the tongue.
Who follow next, a double danger bring,
Not only hating David, but the king;
The Solymaean rout; well vers'd of old
In godly faction, and in treason bold;
Cow'ring and quaking at a conqu'ror's sword,
But lofty to a lawful prince restor'd;
Saw with disdain an Ethnic plot begun,
And scorn'd by Jebusites to be out–done.
Hot Levites headed these; who pull'd before
From th'Ark, which in the Judges' days they bore,

Resum'd their Cant, and with a zealous cry,
Pursu'd their old belov'd Theocracy.
Where Sanhedrin and Priest enslav'd the nation,
And justifi'd their spoils by inspiration:
For who so fit for reign as Aaron's race,
If once dominion they could found in Grace?
These led the pack; though not of surest scent,
Yet deepest mouth'd against the government.
A numerous host of dreaming saints succeed;
Of the true old enthusiastic breed:
'Gainst form and order they their pow'r employ;
Nothing to build, and all things to destroy.
But far more numerous was the herd of such,
Who think too little, and who talk too much.
These, out of mere instinct, they knew not why,
Ador'd their father's God, and property:
And by the same blind benefit of fate,
The Devil and the Jebusite did hate:
Born to be saved even in their own despite;
Because they could not help believing right.
Such were the tools; but a whole Hydra more
Remains, of sprouting heads too long, to score.
Some of their chiefs were princes of the land:
In the first rank of these did Zimri stand:
A man so various, that he seem'd to be
Not one, but all Mankind's Epitome.
Stiff in opinions, always in the wrong;
Was everything by starts, and nothing long:
But in the course of one revolving moon,
Was chemist, fiddler, statesman, and buffoon:
Then all for women, painting, rhyming, drinking;
Besides ten thousand freaks that died in thinking.
Blest madman, who could every hour employ,
With something new to wish, or to enjoy!
Railing and praising were his usual themes;
And both (to show his judgment) in extremes:

16

So over violent, or over civil,
That every man, with him, was god or devil.
In squandering wealth was his peculiar art:
Nothing went unrewarded, but desert.
Beggar'd by fools, whom still he found too late:
He had his jest, and they had his estate.
He laugh'd himself from court; then sought relief
By forming parties, but could ne'er be chief:
For, spite of him, the weight of business fell
On Absalom and wise Achitophel:
Thus, wicked but in will, of means bereft,
He left not faction, but of that was left.

Titles and names 'twere tedious to rehearse
Of lords, below the dignity of verse.
Wits, warriors, commonwealths—men, were the best:
Kind husbands and mere nobles all the rest.
And, therefore in the name of dullness, be
The well—hung Balaam and cold Caleb free.
And canting Nadab let oblivion damn,
Who made new porridge for the Paschal Lamb.
Let friendship's holy band some names assure:
Some their own worth, and some let scorn secure.
Nor shall the rascal rabble here have place,
Whom kings no titles gave, and God no grace:
Not bull—faced Jonas, who could statutes draw
To mean rebellion, and make treason law.
But he, though bad, is follow'd by a worse,
The wretch, who Heav'n's Anointed dar'd to curse.
Shimei, whose youth did early promise bring
Of zeal to God, and hatred to his king;
Did wisely from expensive sins refrain,
And never broke the Sabbath, but for gain:
Nor ever was he known an oath to vent,
Or curse, unless against the government.
Thus, heaping wealth, by the most ready way

Among the Jews, which was to cheat and pray;
The city, to reward his pious hate
Against his master, chose him magistrate:
His hand a vare of justice did uphold;
His neck was loaded with a chain of gold.
During his office, treason was no crime.
The sons of Belial had a glorious time:
For Shimei, though not prodigal of pelf,
Yet lov'd his wicked neighbour as himself:
When two or three were gather'd to declaim
Against the monarch of Jerusalem,
Shimei was always in the midst of them.
And, if they curst the king when he was by,
Would rather curse, than break good company.
If any durst his factious friends accuse,
He pack'd a jury of dissenting Jews:
Whose fellow–feeling, in the godly cause,
Would free the suff'ring saint from human laws.
For laws are only made to punish those
Who serve the king, and to protect his foes.
If any leisure time he had from pow'r,
(Because 'tis sin to mis–employ an hour;)
His bus'ness was, by writing, to persuade,
That kings were useless, and a clog to trade:
And, that his noble style he might refine,
No Rechabite more shunn'd the fumes of wine.
Chaste were his cellars; and his shrieval board
The grossness of a city feast abhorr'd:
His cooks, with long disuse, their trade forgot;
Cool was his kitchen, though his brains were hot.
Such frugal virtue malice may accuse;
But sure 'twas necessary to the Jews:
For towns once burnt, such magistrates require
As dare not tempt God's providence by fire.
With spiritual food he fed his servants well,
But free from flesh, that made the Jews rebel:

And Moses' laws he held in more account
For forty days of fasting in the mount.
To speak the rest, who better are forgot,
Would tire a well–breath'd witness of the plot:
Yet, Corah, thou shalt from oblivion pass;
Erect thyself thou monumental brass:
High as the serpent of thy metal made,
While nations stand secure beneath thy shade.
What though his birth were base, yet comets rise
From earthy vapours e'er they shine in skies.
Prodigious actions may as well be done
By weaver's issue, as by prince's son.
This arch–attestor, for the public good,
By that one deed ennobles all his blood.
Who ever ask'd the witnesses' high race,
Whose oath with martyrdom did Stephen grace?
Ours was a Levite, and as times went then,
His tribe were God–almighty's gentlemen.
Sunk were his eyes, his voice was harsh and loud,
Sure signs he neither choleric was, nor proud:
His long chin prov'd his wit; his saint–like grace
A church vermilion, and a Moses' face.
His memory, miraculously great,
Could plots exceeding man's belief, repeat;
Which therefore cannot be accounted lies,
For human wit could never such devise.
Some future truths are mingled in his book;
But, where the witness fail'd, the Prophet spoke:
Some things like visionary flights appear;
The spirit caught him up, the Lord knows where:
And gave him his rabbinical degree,
Unknown to foreign university.
His judgment yet his mem'ry did excel:
Which piec'd his wondrous evidence so well:
And suited to the temper of the times;
Then groaning under Jebusitic crimes.

Let Israel's foes suspect his Heav'nly call,
And rashly judge his writ apocryphal;
Our laws for such affronts have forfeits made:
He takes his life, who takes away his trade.
Were I myself in witness Corah's place,
The wretch who did me such a dire disgrace,
Should whet my memory, though once forgot,
To make him an appendix of my plot.
His zeal to Heav'n made him his prince despise,
And load his person with indignities:
But Zeal peculiar privilege affords,
Indulging latitude to deeds and words.
And Corah might for Agag's murther call,
In terms as coarse as Samuel us'd to Saul.
What others in his evidence did join,
(The best that could be had for love or coin,)
In Corah's own predicament will fall:
For Witness is a common name to all.

Surrounded thus with friends of every sort,
Deluded Absalom forsakes the court:
Impatient of high hopes, urg'd with renown,
And fir'd with near possession of a crown:
Th' admiring crowd are dazzled with surprise,
And on his goodly person feed their eyes:
His joy conceal'd, he sets himself to show;
On each side bowing popularly low:
His looks, his gestures, and his words he frames,
And with familiar ease repeats their names.
Thus, form'd by Nature, furnish'd out with arts,
He glides unfelt into their secret hearts:
Then, with a kind compassionating look,
And sighs, bespeaking pity e'er he spoke:
Few words he said; but easy those and fit:
More slow than Hybla drops, and far more sweet.

I mourn, my country–men, your lost estate;
Though far unable to prevent your fate:
Behold a banish'd man, for your dear cause
Expos'd a prey to arbitrary laws!
Yet oh! that I alone could be undone,
Cut off from empire, and no more a son!
Now all your liberties a spoil are made;
Egypt and Tyrus intercept your trade,
And Jebusites your sacred rites invade.
My father, whom with reverence yet I name,
Charm'd into ease, is careless of his fame:
And, brib'd with petty sums of foreign gold,
Is grown in Bathsheba's embraces old:
Exalts his enemies, his friends destroys:
And all his pow'r against himself employs.
He gives, and let him give my right away:
But why should he his own, and yours betray?
He, only he can make the nation bleed,
And he alone from my revenge is freed.
Take then my tears (with that he wip'd his eyes)
'Tis all the aid my present pow'r supplies:
No court–informer can these arms accuse;
These arms may sons against their fathers use;
And, 'tis my wish, the next successor's reign
May make no other Israelite complain.

Youth, beauty, graceful action, seldom fail:
But common interest always will prevail:
And pity never ceases to be shown
To him, who makes the people's wrongs his own.
The crowd, (that still believe their kings oppress,)
With lifted hands their young Messiah bless:
Who now begins his progress to ordain;
With chariots, horsemen, and a num'rous train:
From East to West his glories he displays:
And, like the sun, the Promis'd Land surveys.

Fame runs before him, as the Morning–Star;
And shouts of joy salute him from afar:
Each house receives him as a guardian God;
And consecrates the place of his abode:
But hospitable treats did most commend
Wise Issachar, his wealthy western friend.
This moving court, that caught the people's eyes,
And seem'd but pomp, did other ends disguise:
Achitophel had form'd it, with intent
To sound the depths, and fathom where it went,
The people's hearts; distinguish friends from foes;
And try their strength, before they came to blows.
Yet all was colour'd with a smooth pretence
Of specious love, and duty to their prince.
Religion, and redress of grievances,
Two names, that always cheat and always please,
Are often urg'd; and good King David's life
Endanger'd by a brother and a wife.
Thus, in a pageant show, a plot is made;
And peace itself is war in masquerade.
Oh foolish Israel! never warn'd by ill:
Still the same bait, and circumvented still!
Did ever men forsake their present ease,
In midst of health imagine a disease;
Take pains contingent mischiefs to foresee,
Make heirs for monarchs, and for God decree?
What shall we think! Can people give away
Both for themselves and sons, their native sway?
Then they are left defenceless to the sword
Of each unbounded arbitrary lord:
And laws are vain, by which we right enjoy,
If kings unquestion'd can those laws destroy.
Yet, if the crowd be judge of fit and just,
And kings are only officers in trust,
Then this resuming cov'nant was declar'd
When Kings were made, or is for ever bar'd:

If those who gave the sceptre could not tie
By their own deed their own posterity,
How then could Adam bind his future race?
How could his forfeit on mankind take place?
Or how could heavenly justice damn us all,
Who ne'er consented to our father's fall?
Then kings are slaves to those whom they command,
And tenants to their people's pleasure stand.
Add, that the pow'r for property allow'd,
Is mischievously seated in the crowd:
For who can be secure of private right,
If sovereign sway may be dissolv'd by might?
Nor is the people's judgment always true:
The most may err as grossly as the few.
And faultless kings run down, by common cry,
For vice, oppression and for tyranny.
What standard is there in a fickle rout,
Which, flowing to the mark, runs faster out?
Nor only crowds, but Sanhedrins may be
Infected with this public lunacy:
And share the madness of rebellious times,
To murther monarchs for imagin'd crimes.
If they may give and take whene'er they please,
Not kings alone, (the godhead's images,)
But government itself at length must fall
To nature's state, where all have right to all.
Yet, grant our lords the people kings can make,
What prudent men a settled throne would shake?
For whatsoe'er their sufferings were before,
That change they covet makes them suffer more.
All other errors but disturb a state;
But innovation is the blow of fate.
If ancient fabrics nod, and threat to fall,
To patch the flaws, and buttress up the wall,
Thus far 'tis duty; but here fix the mark:
For all beyond it is to touch our Ark.

To change foundations, cast the frame anew,
Is work for rebels who base ends pursue:
At once divine and human laws control;
And mend the parts by ruin of the whole.
The tamp'ring world is subject to this curse,
To physic their disease into a worse.

Now what relief can righteous David bring?
How fatal 'tis to be too good a king!
Friends he has few, so high the madness grows;
Who dare be such, must be the people's foes:
Yet some there were, ev'n in the worst of days;
Some let me name, and naming is to praise.

In this short file Barzillai first appears;
Barzillai crown'd with honour and with years:
Long since, the rising rebels he withstood
In regions waste, beyond the Jordan's flood:
Unfortunately brave to buoy the state;
But sinking underneath his master's fate:
In exile with his god–like prince he mourn'd:
For him he suffer'd, and with him return'd.
The court he practis'd, not the courtier's art:
Large was his wealth, but larger was his heart:
Which well the noblest objects knew to choose,
The fighting warrior, and recording Muse.
His bed could once a fruitful issue boast:
Now more than half a father's name is lost.
His eldest hope, with every grace adorn'd,
By me (so Heav'n will have it) always mourn'd,
And always honour'd, snatch'd in manhood's prime
B' unequal Fates, and Providence's crime:
Yet not before the goal of honour won,
All parts fulfill'd, of subject and of son;
Swift was the race, but short the time to run.
Oh narrow circle, but of pow'r divine,

24

Scanted in space, but perfect in thy line!
By sea, by land, thy matchless worth was known;
Arms thy delight, and war was all thy own:
Thy force infus'd, the fainting Tyrians propp'd:
And haughty Pharaoh found his fortune stopp'd.
Oh ancient honour, Oh unconquer'd Hand,
Whom foes unpunish'd never could withstand!
But Israel was unworthy of thy name:
Short is the date of all immoderate fame.
It looks as Heav'n our ruin had design'd,
And durst not trust thy fortune and thy mind.
Now, free from earth, thy disencumber'd Soul
Mounts up, and leaves behind the clouds and starry pole:
From thence thy kindred legions may'st thou bring,
To aid the Guardian Angel of thy king.
Here stop my Muse, here cease thy painful flight;
No pinions can pursue immortal height:
Tell good Barzillai thou canst sing no more,
And tell thy soul she should have fled before;
Or fled she with his life, and left this verse
To hang on her departed patron's hearse?
Now take thy steepy flight from Heav'n, and see
If thou canst find on earth another he;
Another he would be too hard to find,
See then whom thou canst see not far behind.
Zadoc the priest whom, shunning, pow'r and place,
His lowly mind advanc'd to David's grace:
With him the Sagan of Jerusalem,
Of hospitable soul and noble stem;
Him of the western dome, whose weighty sense
Flows in fit words and heavenly eloquence.
The Prophet's sons by such example led,
To learning and to loyalty were bred:
For colleges on bounteous kings depend,
And never rebel was to arts a friend.
To these succeed the pillars of the laws,

Who best could plead, and best can judge a cause.
Next them a train of loyal peers ascend:
Sharp judging Adriel, the Muse's friend,
Himself a Muse:—in Sanhedrin's debate
True to his prince; but not a slave of state.
Whom David's love with honours did adorn,
That from his disobedient son were torn.
Jotham of piercing wit and pregnant thought,
Endow'd by Nature, and by learning taught
To move assemblies, who but only tri'd
The worse awhile, then chose the better side;
Nor chose alone, but turn'd the balance too;
So much the weight of one brave man can do.
Hushai, the friend of David in distress,
In public storms of manly steadfastness;
By foreign treaties he inform'd his youth;
And join'd experience to his native truth.
His frugal care suppli'd the wanting throne;
Frugal for that, but bounteous of his own:
'Tis easy conduct when exchequers flow;
But hard the task to manage well the low:
For sovereign power is too depress'd or high,
When kings are forc'd to sell, or crowds to buy.
Indulge one labour more, my weary Muse,
For Amiel, who can Amiel's praise refuse?
Of ancient race by birth, but nobler yet
In his own worth, and without title great:
The Sanhedrin long time as chief he rul'd,
Their reason guided, and their passion cool'd;
So dext'rous was he in the crown's defence,
So form'd to speak a loyal nation's sense,
That as their band was Israel's tribes in small,
So fit was he to represent them all.
Now rasher charioteers the seat ascend,
Whose loose careers his steady skill commend:
They, like th'unequal ruler of the day,

Misguide the seasons and mistake the way;
While he withdrawn at their mad labour smiles,
And safe enjoys the sabbath of his toils.

These were the chief; a small but faithful band
Of worthies, in the breach who dar'd to stand,
And tempt th'united fury of the land.
With grief they view'd such powerful engines bent,
To batter down the lawful government.
A numerous faction with pretended frights,
In Sanhedrins to plume the regal rights.
The true successor from the court remov'd:
The plot, by hireling witnesses, improv'd.
These ills they saw, and as their duty bound,
They show'd the king the danger of the wound:
That no concessions from the throne would please;
But lenitives fomented the disease:
That Absalom, ambitious of the crown,
Was made the lure to draw the people down:
That false Achitophel's pernicious hate,
Had turn'd the plot to ruin church and state:
The Council violent, the rabble worse:
That Shimei taught Jerusalem to curse.

With all these loads of injuries opprest,
And long revolving in his careful breast
Th'event of things; at last his patience tir'd,
Thus from his royal throne, by Heav'n inspir'd,
The god–like David spoke; and awful fear
His train their Maker in their Master hear.

Thus long have I by native mercy sway'd,
My wrongs dissembl'd, my revenge delay'd:
So willing to forgive th'offending age;
So much the father did the king assuage.
But now so far my clemency they slight,

Th' offenders question my forgiving right.
That one was made for many, they contend:
But 'tis to rule, for that's a monarch's end.
They call my tenderness of blood, my fear:
Though manly tempers can the longest bear.
Yet, since they will divert my native course,
'Tis time to shew I am not good by force.
Those heap'd affronts that haughty subjects bring,
Are burdens for a camel, not a king:
Kings are the public pillars of the state,
Born to sustain and prop the nation's weight:
If my young Sampson will pretend a call
To shake the column, let him share the fall:
But oh that yet he would repent and live!
How easy 'tis for parents to forgive!
With how few tears a pardon might be won
From Nature, pleading for a darling son!
Poor pitied youth, by my paternal care,
Rais'd up to all the heights his frame could bear:
Had God ordain'd his fate for empire born,
He would have giv'n his soul another turn:
Gull'd with a patriot's name, whose modern sense
Is one that would by law supplant his prince:
The people's brave, the politician's tool;
Never was patriot yet, but was a fool.
Whence comes it that religion and the laws
Should more be Absalom's than David's cause?
His old instructor, e'er he lost his place,
Was never thought endued with so much grace.
Good heav'ns, how faction can a patriot paint!
My rebel ever proves my people's saint;
Would they impose an heir upon the throne?
Let Sanhedrins be taught to give their own.
A king's at least a part of government;
And mine as requisite as their consent:
Without my leave a future king to choose,

Infers a right the present to depose;
True, they petition me t'approve their choice:
But Esau's hands suit ill with Jacob's voice.
My pious subjects for my safety pray,
Which to secure they take my pow'r away.
From plots and treasons Heav'n preserve my years
But save me most from my petitioners.
Unsatiate as the barren womb or grave;
God cannot grant so much as they can crave.
What then is left but with a jealous eye
To guard the small remains of royalty?
The law shall still direct my peaceful sway,
And the same law teach rebels to obey:
Votes shall no more establish'd pow'r control,
Such votes as make a part exceed the whole:
No groundless clamours shall my friends remove,
Nor crowds have pow'r to punish ere they prove:
For gods, and god–like kings their care express,
Still to defend their servants in distress.
Oh that my pow'r to saving were confin'd:
Why am I forc'd, like Heav'n, against my mind,
To make examples of another kind?
Must I at length the sword of justice draw?
Oh curst effects of necessary law!
How ill my fear they by my mercy scan,
Beware the fury of a patient man.
Law they require, let law then show her face;
They could not be content to look on grace,
Her hinder parts, but with a daring eye
To tempt the terror of her front, and die.
By their own arts 'tis righteously decreed,
Those dire artificers of death shall bleed.
Against themselves their witnesses will swear,
Till viper–like their mother plot they tear:
And suck for nutriment that bloody gore
Which was their principle of life before.

Their Belial with the Belzebub will fight;
Thus on my foes, my foes shall do me right:
Nor doubt th'event: for factious crowds engage
In their first onset, all their brutal rage;
Then, let 'em take an unresisted course:
Retire and traverse, and delude their force:
But when they stand all breathless, urge the fight,
And rise upon 'em with redoubled might:
For lawful pow'r is still superior found,
When long driv'n back, at length it stands the ground.

He said. Th' Almighty, nodding, gave consent;
And peals of thunder shook the firmament.
Henceforth a series of new time began,
The mighty years in long procession ran:
Once more the god–like David was restor'd,
And willing nations knew their lawful lord.

MAC FLECKNOE: A SATIRE UPON THE TRUE–BLUE PROTESTANT POET T.S.

All human things are subject to decay,
And, when Fate summons, monarchs must obey:
This Flecknoe found, who, like Augustus, young
Was call'd to empire, and had govern'd long:
In prose and verse, was own'd, without dispute
Through all the realms of Non–sense, absolute.
This aged prince now flourishing in peace,
And blest with issue of a large increase,
Worn out with business, did at length debate
To settle the succession of the State:
And pond'ring which of all his sons was fit
To reign, and wage immortal war with wit;

30

Cry'd, 'tis resolv'd; for nature pleads that he
Should only rule, who most resembles me:
Shadwell alone my perfect image bears,
Mature in dullness from his tender years.
Shadwell alone, of all my sons, is he
Who stands confirm'd in full stupidity.
The rest to some faint meaning make pretence,
But Shadwell never deviates into sense.
Some beams of wit on other souls may fall,
Strike through and make a lucid interval;
But Shadwell's genuine night admits no ray,
His rising fogs prevail upon the day:
Besides his goodly fabric fills the eye,
And seems design'd for thoughtless majesty:
Thoughtless as monarch oaks, that shade the plain,
And, spread in solemn state, supinely reign.
Heywood and Shirley were but types of thee,
Thou last great prophet of tautology:
Even I, a dunce of more renown than they,
Was sent before but to prepare thy way;
And coarsely clad in Norwich drugget came
To teach the nations in thy greater name.
My warbling lute, the lute I whilom strung
When to King John of Portugal I sung,
Was but the prelude to that glorious day,
When thou on silver Thames did'st cut thy way,
With well tim'd oars before the royal barge,
Swell'd with the pride of thy celestial charge;
And big with hymn, commander of an host,
The like was ne'er in Epsom blankets toss'd.
Methinks I see the new Arion sail,
The lute still trembling underneath thy nail.
At thy well sharpen'd thumb from shore to shore
The treble squeaks for fear, the basses roar:
Echoes from Pissing–Alley, Shadwell call,
And Shadwell they resound from Aston Hall.

31

About thy boat the little fishes throng,
As at the morning toast, that floats along.
Sometimes as prince of thy harmonious band
Thou wield'st thy papers in thy threshing hand.
St. Andre's feet ne'er kept more equal time,
Not ev'n the feet of thy own Psyche's rhyme:
Though they in number as in sense excel;
So just, so like tautology they fell,
That, pale with envy, Singleton forswore
The lute and sword which he in triumph bore
And vow'd he ne'er would act Villerius more.
Here stopt the good old sire; and wept for joy
In silent raptures of the hopeful boy.
All arguments, but most his plays, persuade,
That for anointed dullness he was made.

Close to the walls which fair Augusta bind,
(The fair Augusta much to fears inclin'd)
An ancient fabric, rais'd t'inform the sight,
There stood of yore, and Barbican it hight:
A watch tower once; but now, so fate ordains,
Of all the pile an empty name remains.
From its old ruins brothel–houses rise,
Scenes of lewd loves, and of polluted joys.
Where their vast courts, the mother–strumpets keep,
And, undisturb'd by watch, in silence sleep.
Near these a nursery erects its head,
Where queens are form'd, and future heroes bred;
Where unfledg'd actors learn to laugh and cry,
Where infant punks their tender voices try,
And little Maximins the gods defy.
Great Fletcher never treads in buskins here,
Nor greater Jonson dares in socks appear;
But gentle Simkin just reception finds
Amidst this monument of vanish'd minds:
Pure clinches, the suburbian muse affords;

And Panton waging harmless war with words.
Here Flecknoe, as a place to fame well known,
Ambitiously design'd his Shadwell's throne.
For ancient Decker prophesi'd long since,
That in this pile should reign a mighty prince,
Born for a scourge of wit, and flail of sense:
To whom true dullness should some Psyches owe,
But worlds of Misers from his pen should flow;
Humorists and hypocrites it should produce,
Whole Raymond families, and tribes of Bruce.

Now Empress Fame had publisht the renown,
Of Shadwell's coronation through the town.
Rous'd by report of fame, the nations meet,
From near Bun–Hill, and distant Watling–street.
No Persian carpets spread th'imperial way,
But scatter'd limbs of mangled poets lay:
From dusty shops neglected authors come,
Martyrs of pies, and reliques of the bum.
Much Heywood, Shirley, Ogleby there lay,
But loads of Shadwell almost chok'd the way.
Bilk'd stationers for yeoman stood prepar'd,
And Herringman was Captain of the Guard.
The hoary prince in majesty appear'd,
High on a throne of his own labours rear'd.
At his right hand our young Ascanius sat
Rome's other hope, and pillar of the state.
His brows thick fogs, instead of glories, grace,
And lambent dullness play'd around his face.
As Hannibal did to the altars come,
Sworn by his sire a mortal foe to Rome;
So Shadwell swore, nor should his vow be vain,
That he till death true dullness would maintain;
And in his father's right, and realm's defence,
Ne'er to have peace with wit, nor truce with sense.
The king himself the sacred unction made,

As king by office, and as priest by trade:
In his sinister hand, instead of ball,
He plac'd a mighty mug of potent ale;
Love's kingdom to his right he did convey,
At once his sceptre and his rule of sway;
Whose righteous lore the prince had practis'd young,
And from whose loins recorded Psyche sprung,
His temples last with poppies were o'er spread,
That nodding seem'd to consecrate his head:
Just at that point of time, if fame not lie,
On his left hand twelve reverend owls did fly.
So Romulus, 'tis sung, by Tiber's brook,
Presage of sway from twice six vultures took.
Th'admiring throng loud acclamations make,
And omens of his future empire take.
The sire then shook the honours of his head,
And from his brows damps of oblivion shed
Full on the filial dullness: long he stood,
Repelling from his breast the raging god;
At length burst out in this prophetic mood:

Heavens bless my son, from Ireland let him reign
To far Barbadoes on the Western main;
Of his dominion may no end be known,
And greater than his father's be his throne.
Beyond love's kingdom let him stretch his pen;
He paus'd, and all the people cry'd Amen.
Then thus, continu'd he, my son advance
Still in new impudence, new ignorance.
Success let other teach, learn thou from me
Pangs without birth, and fruitless industry.
Let Virtuosos in five years be writ;
Yet not one thought accuse thy toil of wit.
Let gentle George in triumph tread the stage,
Make Dorimant betray, and Loveit rage;
Let Cully, Cockwood, Fopling, charm the pit,

34

And in their folly show the writer's wit.
Yet still thy fools shall stand in thy defence,
And justify their author's want of sense.
Let 'em be all by thy own model made
Of dullness, and desire no foreign aid:
That they to future ages may be known,
Not copies drawn, but issue of thy own.
Nay let thy men of wit too be the same,
All full of thee, and differing but in name;
But let no alien Sedley interpose
To lard with wit thy hungry Epsom prose.
And when false flowers of rhetoric thou would'st cull,
Trust Nature, do not labour to be dull;
But write thy best, and top; and in each line,
Sir Formal's oratory will be thine.
Sir Formal, though unsought, attends thy quill,
And does thy Northern Dedications fill.
Nor let false friends seduce thy mind to fame,
By arrogating Jonson's hostile name.
Let Father Flecknoe fire thy mind with praise,
And Uncle Ogleby thy envy raise.
Thou art my blood, where Jonson has no part;
What share have we in Nature or in Art?
Where did his wit on learning fix a brand,
And rail at arts he did not understand?
Where made he love in Prince Nicander's vein,
Or swept the dust in Psyche's humble strain?
Where sold he bargains, whip–stitch, kiss my arse,
Promis'd a play and dwindled to a farce?
When did his muse from Fletcher scenes purloin,
As thou whole Eth'ridge dost transfuse to thine?
But so transfus'd as oil on waters flow,
His always floats above, thine sinks below.
This is thy province, this thy wondrous way,
New humours to invent for each new play:
This is that boasted bias of thy mind,

By which one way, to dullness, 'tis inclin'd,
Which makes thy writings lean on one side still,
And in all changes that way bends thy will.
Nor let thy mountain belly make pretence
Of likeness; thine's a tympany of sense.
A tun of man in thy large bulk is writ,
But sure thou 'rt but a kilderkin of wit.
Like mine thy gentle numbers feebly creep,
Thy Tragic Muse gives smiles, thy Comic sleep.
With whate'er gall thou sett'st thy self to write,
Thy inoffensive satires never bite.
In thy felonious heart, though venom lies,
It does but touch thy Irish pen, and dies.
Thy genius calls thee not to purchase fame
In keen iambics, but mild anagram:
Leave writing plays, and choose for thy command
Some peaceful province in acrostic land.
There thou may'st wings display and altars raise,
And torture one poor word ten thousand ways.
Or if thou would'st thy diff'rent talents suit,
Set thy own songs, and sing them to thy lute.
He said, but his last words were scarcely heard,
For Bruce and Longvil had a trap prepar'd,
And down they sent the yet declaiming bard.
Sinking he left his drugget robe behind,
Born upwards by a subterranean wind.
The mantle fell to the young prophet's part,
With double portion of his father's art.

TO THE MEMORY OF MR. OLDHAM

Farewell, too little and too lately known,
Whom I began to think and call my own;
For sure our souls were near ally'd; and thine
Cast in the same poetic mould with mine.

One common note on either lyre did strike,
And knaves and fools we both abhorr'd alike:
To the same goal did both our studies drive,
The last set out the soonest did arrive.
Thus Nisus fell upon the slippery place,
While his young friend perform'd and won the race.
O early ripe! to thy abundant store
What could advancing age have added more?
It might (what nature never gives the young)
Have taught the numbers of thy native tongue.
But satire needs not those, and wit will shine
Through the harsh cadence of a rugged line.
A noble error, and but seldom made,
When poets are by too much force betray'd.
Thy generous fruits, though gather'd ere their prime
Still show'd a quickness; and maturing time
But mellows what we write to the dull sweets of rhyme.
Once more, hail and farewell; farewell thou young,
But ah too short, Marcellus of our tongue;
Thy brows with ivy, and with laurels bound;
But fate and gloomy night encompass thee around.

Printed in the United Kingdom
by Lightning Source UK Ltd.
111903UKS00002B/11

9 781419 131844